BUSINESS ANALYST'S MENTOR BOOK

EMRAH YAYICI

ISBN: 978-605-86037-1-4

About The Author

Emrah Yayici is the managing partner of BA-Works, Keytorc and UXservices. He started his career as a technology consultant at Arthur Andersen and Accenture. Afterward he led global enterprise transformation projects at Beko-Grundig Electronics.

During his career he has managed multinational and cross-functional project teams in banking, insurance, telecommunications, media, consumer electronics, and IT industries.

He is now sharing his experience about business analysis, software testing, user experience design, and usability testing by publishing articles and books and by speaking at conferences.

He is contributing to IIBA® (International Institute of Business Analysis) as a local chapter president. He also contributed to ISTQB® (International Software Testing Board) as former international board member.

Preface

Business Analyst's Mentor Book includes tips and best practices in a broad range of topics like:

- business analysis career
- business analysis skills
- requirements gathering and documentation
- scope management
- change request management
- conflict management
- use cases
- UML
- agile and waterfall methodologies
- user interface design
- usability testing
- software testing
- automation tools.

Real-life examples are provided to help readers apply these tips and best practices in their own IT organizations.

The approach presented in the book can also be used by IT managers in transforming the software requirements management process at their companies.

Table of Contents

1. Which Skills Are Important for a Successful Career in Business Analysis?

Business analysis profession requires business domain knowledge and technical skills combined with multidisciplinary competencies.

Have a Bird's-Eye View

The key success factor in business analysis is the ability to prevent scope creep, which is the number one reason for project failures. Business analysts should have the ability to see the big picture and have a holistic view of the requirements to best manage the scope.

Don't Escalate Everything

Business analysis (also known as requirements management) has the characteristics of a managerial role more than an operational one. Managerial roles require taking initiative when needed. As a result, business analysts should not escalate every problem to their upper management before trying hard to solve problems themselves. While feeling trapped in this situation, they should remember the famous quotation from American scientist and author Dr. James Jay Horning: "Good judgment comes from experience. Experience comes from bad judgment."

Learn Sales 101

Although business analysts don't sell any products or services, they still need sales and marketing skills to better express and promote their ideas during negotiations with other project stakeholders.

The underlying principle in Sales 101 is "people don't like someone trying to sell something to them; however, they like the experience of buying something." If this fact is true, then the most basic rule in sales should be to stimulate the buying desire of people instead of pushing them to buy something. This happens when people realize the value of an offering, feel jealous of not having it when someone else already has, or are afraid of losing something because of not having it. For example, if people from business units resist the implementation of a new software, business analysts can persuade them by doing the following: proving the new software's value add compared to the legacy system (showing value), giving examples about good practices of its similar use and gained benefits at competitors (making them feel jealous), and proving the opportunity cost of not implementing the new software on time (making them afraid of not having it).

Learn to Speak with Professional Jargon

Compared to developers and testers, business analysts usually have more difficulty in describing and promoting the work they have done.

For example, if a manager requests information from a developer about his daily work, the developer may respond as: "Today I have completed the coding of fifteen Java classes, worked on XML files to integrate middleware software, and optimized the query structure in the database." The manager will probably reply, "Thanks, good work!"

If the same manager asks the same question to a tester, she may respond as: "Today I have run twenty test cases covering 5 percent of requirements, found fifteen high-priority defects, and completed the keyword-driven regression test scripts on the test automation tool." Again, the manager will probably reply, "Wow, good work!"

If the same question is asked to the business analyst, he will respond as: "Today I had a long meeting with the business unit. As usual, we had conflicts about many issues. We conducted a second follow-up meeting with the participation of other stakeholders to discuss these issues. Afterward I started to prepare analysis documents for business units' approval." The manager usually replies as: "OK, please keep me informed about the status of conflicts; we are running out of time!"

If business analysts speak with professional jargon, it will be easier for them to express their hard work in a more effective way. In the previous dialogue, the business analyst could reply as: "Today I have done a focus group meeting with the business unit to define user requirements and business rules. In the afternoon we conducted a workshop session with the participation of other relevant business units to resolve integration issues. After that meeting we defined functional and non-functional requirements in the use case document format and prepared activity diagrams for complex scenarios. Now I will update the traceability matrix and send the requirements documents for sign-off." This time the business analyst will have more chance to impress and convince the manager about his progress. Another benefit of using professional jargon is that it promotes speaking the same language within the IT organization.

Keep Your Learning Curve Always Upward

"Most of the time the goal of computer science is to build something that will last at least until we've finished building it." As mentioned in this anonymous quotation, the dynamic structure of information technologies and business models in every industry pushes companies and professionals to have an updated knowledge base.

To have a rising professional career, business analysts should have a continuous upward learning curve. Being active in chapters of professional organizations, following latest trends and practices published in software engineering magazines, and participating at professional conferences will support this self-improvement process.

2. What Should the Level of Technical Skills Be for Business Analysts?

```
tring sql = "select * from st
resultSet = statement.executeQu
if (resultSet.next()) {
  result = true;
  setStoreId(resultSet.getInt("s
  storeDescription = res
  storeTypeId = r
  storeAdd
```

Business analysts are not only hired from computer engineering graduates but also from other departments that have limited technical and software engineering knowledge, such as management, industrial engineering, mathematics, and statistics.

Besides new graduates there are many people from business units who are transferred to business analysis teams due to their domain knowledge but who have limited or no software engineering knowledge.

Business vs. IT Centricity

For either the new graduate or the experienced professional, lack of technical skills becomes the main concern of all newly hired business analysts. In addition to their business knowledge, business analysts know that they must also gain IT skills to be successful as the bridge between business units and developers.

But the main question is whether to be more business or IT centric.

A business analyst's main responsibility is to transform business needs into requirements. Hence they should definitely be business centric to find the answers of "Why to implement this system" (to define business requirements), "What the system does" (to define functional requirements), and "How the system works" (to define non-functional requirements, business rules, and assumptions) questions by working with business units.

On the other hand, business analysts are also responsible for communicating requirements to developers, which requires IT centricity. The level of their IT centricity depends on the answer of whether or not business analysts should also be responsible for asking the "Technically How the system does" question.

A Separate Role: System Analysts

The answer to this question depends on the existence of a separate role in the company called system analyst. System analysts are responsible for answering the "Technically How" question and defining system requirements. They work on technical issues like software architecture and data models by using modeling techniques such as UML (Unified Modeling Language) and BPEL (Business Process Execution Language).

If a separate system analysis team exists in the company or this role is completely assigned to developers, then business analysts should be 80 percent business centric and 20 percent IT centric. But if the system analysis role is completely assigned to business analysts, then analysts should be 50 percent business centric and 50 percent IT centric.

Twenty percent IT centricity does not require advanced technical skills like writing source code, database programming with PLSQL, or creating XML web services. But it requires basic IT knowledge like knowing what "class" and "relationship" mean in object-oriented development and abilities like writing simple SQL queries on RDBMSs (relational database management systems).

Evaluating the technical feasibility of the business unit's requests during requirements gathering sessions is a responsibility of business analysts. Twenty percent IT centricity will be enough to make high-level evaluations and ask the right questions to developers to clarify technical constraints.

In one of our CRM (customer relationship management) projects at a telecommunications company, the marketing manager made a request about campaign management module. He stated that when a customer made an inbound call, the call center application could automatically display his segment and the associated campaign. This meant that if a customer wanted to change his telco operator, the system could predict this and propose him a royalty campaign to prevent his churn. Similarly, the system could also detect up-sell and cross-sell opportunities and offer them to the right people. Since the business analyst in charge of campaign management module did not have enough IT knowledge, he accepted the request of the marketing manager without questioning its technical feasibility. When the analysis documents were reviewed by developers, they told that they needed eight additional months to fulfill these requirements, because a data mining system must also be put in place to be able to make the requested predictive customer segmentations. The extra time and budget needed for the data mining system was not approved by the project manager because it was not planned in the scope of the project. The business analyst had to update the analysis documents and explain this situation to the marketing manager. The manager was disappointed after hearing the rejection of his previously accepted request. This situation could have been managed much better if the business analyst has been more IT centric. In this case he could have realized the necessity of a data mining system during the elicitation meeting and explained the infeasibility of the request to the marketing manager.

IT centricity of business analysts is also important in communications with developers. In the same CRM project, another analyst who was more IT centric was responsible for designing user interfaces. In the design of a campaign definition form, she used a combo box to select customer segments. But the developer proposed that using an option box would be technically easier for him. The business analyst suggested that the developer could easily create an updatable combo box by using web services that would prevent the need for changing the form after each new customer segment was added. The developer also verified her reason and moved forward with this more appropriate design.

Analysts can improve their IT skills by increasing their collaboration with developers in the projects. They should invite developers into requirements review meetings and question the rationale for each technical constraint mentioned by them during these reviews.

3. Is the Business Analyst Role a Good Choice for My Career?

"What appear to us as motions of the sun arise not from its motion but from the motion of the earth and our sphere, with which we revolve about the sun like any other planet." – Copernicus.

After the acceptance of Copernicus's theory, people perceived the sun as the center of the planets in the solar system. This was a paradigm shift in the mindset of human beings who used to envision the earth as the center of the universe throughout history.

In recent years a similar change has also occurred in IT business.

Previously the legacy systems at companies didn't have an open architecture. It was not easy to update them or add new components. Although these systems were highly reliable, they allowed limited changes. Most of the business unit requests could not be fulfilled due to technical constraints. As a result business was mostly driven by IT.

However, due to fierce competition and dynamic business environments in every industry, business units focused on differentiating their products and services by fully benefiting from technology. They became more demanding of IT departments. This fact increased the need for more flexible IT systems, which led to the advent of new software development approaches like object-oriented programming and SOA (service-oriented architectures). Software started to be developed with an open architecture of integrated components. This new way of software development brought more flexibility to IT systems, which meant more tolerance to fulfill business requests.

In this new approach, the most important success factor became achieving seamless orchestration of integrated system components. This required utilization of modeling techniques like UML (Unified Modeling Language), BPMN (Business Process Model and Notation), and BPEL (Business Process Execution Language) as a major part of the software analysis and design profession. This factor increased the strategic importance of business and system analysis in parallel.

Evolution of Enterprise Architecture Role

In this new, more flexible, and productive model, CIOs (chief information officers) need more assistance in keeping the IT architecture of the company aligned with the current and target business architectures. The role in charge of this assistance is defined as "enterprise architect." Enterprise architects are not system architects who design the architecture of IT solutions. Their goal is more holistic and at company level. Enterprise architects are responsible for linking business, information, application, and infrastructure architectures of the company by using frameworks like Togaf and Zachman. They work in coordination with company executives to understand business strategies, evaluate business unit needs against these strategies, and steer technical teams in building sustainable solutions that meet today's and tomorrow's business needs.

Stepping Stone for CIO Position

The enterprise architect profession requires business knowledge, technical skills, and the ability to see the big picture with a bird's-eye view. Hence the most suitable people to fill enterprise architecture positions are experienced business analysts and project managers who naturally gain these competencies as part of their profession. Since enterprise architects are the best candidates to be tomorrow's CIOs, this position is also a good stepping stone for business analysts and project managers. Success in daily business analysis activities like requirements elicitation and documentation is not enough to move forward in this challenging career path. Business analysts should also be involved in strategic tasks like business case development, follow the latest trends and developments in IT technologies, and learn the overall business architecture of their company by working for projects at different business domains.

4. What Is the Relationship between Business Analysis and Project Management?

Regarding their roles and responsibilities, business analysts usually ask the following questions:

- Are we responsible for product scope definition and CR (change request) management?

  Answer: Yes

- Are we responsible for organizing requirements elicitation meetings and managing conflicts?

  Answer: Yes

After getting the "Yes" answers, their next question is: Why do we need project managers?

Let's answer these questions in more detail:

Scope and CR Management

Project manager and business analyst roles have many intersection points. Scope management is one of them. While the project manager is responsible for "project" scope management, the business analysts are responsible for "product" scope management. *Project scope* is defined as the work that needs to be accomplished to deliver a product with specified features, whereas *product scope* represents the features of the product to meet the business needs of the project. Therefore, in order to determine the project scope correctly, the project manager should assist business analysts in defining a clear and correct product scope.

After business analysts reach an agreement with business units about product scope and prepare the business case or vision and scope document, the project manager should define the project scope on the project charter document.

Outputs vs. Outcomes

In addition to project scope management, time and cost management are the other critical knowledge areas in project management. New project managers are first assigned to small-scale projects. If they can complete these projects within time and budget constraints, they are assigned to manage a larger-scale project. If they continue to deliver these large-scale projects on time and with compliance to budget, then they are promoted. Sometimes the pressure to meet time and budget targets can lead project managers to focus more on generating outputs (deliverables) instead of outcomes (value). However, if the requirements cannot be met, the project won't be successful even if it is completed on time and within budget constraints. People always look at the final score instead of how one played during the game.

To prevent this "output" trap and assure the delivery of value-adding "outcomes," project managers should always work in collaboration with business analysts for the correct and complete definition of requirements.

Manage the Project in the Field

Some project managers spend most of their time at the project management office instead of being in the field. At this office they spend most of their time analyzing project status reports. They rarely review requirements documents, user interface designs, and technical specifications. They organize analysis meetings with business units and developers on behalf of business analysts. But, they usually don't attend these meetings, even the most important requirements elicitation workshops. This is not a successful way to manage projects.

Business analysts should organize the requirements gathering meetings themselves. If they have difficulty in meeting business unit representatives, they should ask for the help of the project manager. The project manager should then get in contact with unit heads and ensure the participation of required people in the meetings. The project manager should also attend the critical meetings where high-priority business and user requirements are discussed. This makes project scope management much easier for them.

Conflicts between business analysts and business units are a part of these meetings. Project managers should assist analysts in resolving these conflicts by using their previous experience. They should track the resolution of remaining high-priority conflicts either by using steering committees or subject matter experts.

The project manager should work together with business analysts during impact analysis, evaluation, and approval of CRs (change requests) from business units.

Business Analysis Is the Best Stepping Stone for Project Management

It is not enough to learn and apply standard project management processes and knowledge areas to manage critical projects. Successful project management requires business and technical knowledge, conflict management, communication and negotiation skills, and the ability to see the big picture. This makes business analysis the best school for project management.

Wait at Least Eight Years to Be a Project Manager

The manager title in project "management" attracts a lot of business analysts. They consider this role an opportunity to be a young manager. However, it is better for business analysts to stay on the execution part of projects as an analyst for a certain period of time. This period should not be less than eight years, which is the minimum time to gain the required skill set needed to be able to manage important projects.

5. How Can We Manage the Challenging IT Requests of Business Units?

Business units always want to get the best IT solution in the shortest time with minimum cost. Applying the following best practices will help solution teams respond to these demands with their limited time and resources:

Good, Fast, Cheap Dilemma

According to the Project Management Triangle, in an IT project you can only achieve two out of three objectives: Good, Fast, and Cheap. It is almost impossible to achieve three of them at the same time. To produce a good product in a very short time will require a lot of high-quality resources and will not be cheap. To produce a high-quality product at minimum cost will take a considerable amount of time. And, a product that is built in a short time with minimum cost will most probably not be a high-quality one. During the project scoping phase, the project manager and business analysts should discuss and convince business units about these trade-offs.

Fair Value Principle

When time to market is the most important criterion, the project should be classified as a "Fast Track" one. In these time-sensitive fast track projects, business analysts and project managers should convince business units to get "must-have" features rather than "nice-to-have" features and try to focus on generating "fair value" outcomes.

Perfect Is the Enemy of Good

When business units insist on nice-to-have features, analysts and project managers should remind them of the famous phrase in Voltaire's poem "La Begueule": "perfect is the enemy of good." The phrase tells that insisting on perfection often results in no improvement at all.

Even in time-sensitive fast track projects business units are always eager to expand the scope of the solution by adding nice-to-have features. In one of our mobile banking application development projects, the proposed solution included a feature that made the application capable of searching and displaying the ATMs nearest to the user. In spite of the tough project schedule, the business unit insisted that the application should also display the number of people waiting in front of each ATM. Business analysts worked hard to convince business units to keep this feature out of scope by explaining the risk of not being able to complete the project on time due to this nice-to-have feature.

Priority Quadrant

Having a formal prioritization process is one of the maturity level indicators of a company's requirements management process. In the lack of a prioritization process, business units feel free to request any feature as if IT has unlimited resources. The business units with the highest political power and the best relationship with IT managers usually get the best place in the queue.

The features requested by business units should be prioritized according to two main criteria: business value and implementation difficulty. Business value depends on alignment to business requirements. The items with high business value and low implementation difficulty should be rated as high priority, while the ones with low business value and high implementation difficulty should be rated as low priority. The rest of the features should be labeled as medium priority and prioritized according to their expected frequency of use and time to market constraints. Medium priority features can be relabeled as high priority if they have high frequency of use and there is enough time to implement them. Otherwise, they move to the low priority quadrant.

Next Release Lie

When business units insist on a feature that is nice to have but hard to develop, business analysts sometimes get rid of these demands by postponing their requests. They say this demand will be handled in the next release although it will not. However, promises are hard to forget. When the so-called feature is not developed in the next release, it damages the relationship between the business unit and the project team. Business analysts and project managers should resolve these conflicts with the help of negotiation and communication skills instead of using this unethical, tricky way.

6. How Should We Manage Business Units' IT System Enhancement/Modification Requests?

Despite all their hard work, most IT departments are blamed for not being able to meet the expectations of business units. Business units criticize IT departments for incomplete and late delivery of their requests. If you search for the root cause of this issue, the main reason appears to be the high number of unplanned requests from business units. These requests mostly consist of enhancements/modifications for the current legacy systems.

The high number of these requests also demotivates business analysts, developers, and project managers because instead of being involved in new and innovative projects, they have to spend their efforts on the current legacy systems.

In our clients, we also witness an overwhelming number of IT enhancement/modification requests. Large-scale banks having one hundred to two hundred projects in their annual master plans have 3.000–4.000 of these types of requests. The following best practices should be in place to manage these requests in a better and more controllable way:

Cheap Car Problem

If the additional cost of IT system enhancement/modification requests is not tracked systematically, the total cost of ownership for legacy systems reaches a very high amount. This creates a weird situation like buying a cheap car whose final cost exceeds an expensive car due to the extra accessories added by time.

Differentiate from CRs

In some companies these requests are classified under the same category with CRs (change requests) and hidden into the budgets allocated for ongoing projects. If an enhancement/modification request comes after the release, it is not a CR anymore. These requests should be classified and tracked separately from CRs.

Differentiate from Maintenance Requests

Sometimes enhancement/modification requests are classified under the same category with maintenance requests. This is also a wrong approach since maintenance is a different category whose aim is to ensure continuous operation of the system rather than to enhance the system's attributes. Each system should have a separate maintenance and enhancement/modification track to identify the best time to totally replace it.

Focus on Innovation

If not managed in a structured way, these huge numbers of IT system enhancement/modification requests result in reduced time for projects that generate innovation and competitiveness. Innovative companies make sure that they allocate at least 20 percent of their time to innovative projects.

Demand Management

IT system enhancement/modification requests should be received, evaluated, and prioritized by a dedicated group. In large-scale companies it should be the enterprise architecture team's responsibility to filter the low-priority requests that are not in alignment with the company's business and IT architectural needs. The requests approved by the enterprise architecture team should then be sent to relevant business analysis teams. If a company has a separate agile team, these requests can be directly assigned to the agile team. Agile methodology is very appropriate for development and implementation of these requests with limited documentation and intense collaboration with business units.

In small- and mid-sized companies, project management offices (PMOs) or a team of experienced business analysts can be responsible for evaluating and filtering these requests. While prioritizing of these requests, the main criteria should be business value, frequency of use, implementation difficulty, and time to market.

The status of these requests should be continuously reviewed. Some of the requests waiting in the pipeline may become obsolete due to changing business conditions. These obsolete requests should be identified and eliminated to optimize the utilization of IT resources.

7. What Is the Best Way to Manage Conflicts with Business Units?

Requirements gathering is the most important phase in a software development project. While it is possible to cook bad food from good ingredients, it is not possible to cook good food from bad ingredients. Similarly, although it is possible to build bad-quality software with well-defined requirements, it is impossible to deliver high-quality software with poor requirements even with the best developers.

The most challenging part of the requirements gathering process is the resolution of conflicts with business units.

The following principles should be applied to resolve conflicts with business units and gather requirements in the most effective way:

First, Focus on Business Needs

Business units are not interested in technical aspects of the software. They don't care which database or programming language will be used. They just want the best solution that will help them in achieving their goals in the easiest and fastest way. Hence during requirements gathering meetings, business analysts should give first priority to translating business needs into correct user requirements. They should focus on resolving the conflicts about these requirements before discussing the technical aspects of the system. Doing the right thing is always more important than doing it right.

Ask the Right Questions

In requirements gathering meetings giving right answers to wrong questions is worse than giving wrong answers to the right questions. Wrong questions mislead the team, generate conflicts, waste project time, and result in failure. Business analysts should prepare simple, objective, and to-the-point questions before these meetings.

Quantum Observer Effect

The way of asking questions in requirements gathering meetings is also important. The "observer effect" in quantum mechanics states that "by the act of watching, the observer affects the observed reality." Similarly, asking questions in a biased way impacts the objectivity of answers from business units during requirements gathering meetings.

Conflict Is Not a Bad Thing

Conflicts with business units should be considered positively during the requirements gathering stage. If these conflicts are not discussed and resolved at this early stage of the project, they will later appear as high-cost CRs (change requests) at the coding and testing phases.

Think Differently

"The problems that exist in the world now cannot be solved by the level of thinking that created them." – Albert Einstein.

To resolve conflicts business analysts and project managers should make paradigm shifts and approach problems from different perspectives. For example, the ultrasonography technique, which is used for visualizing subcutaneous body structures by using sound waves, was discovered with a similar approach. Although sound waves were normally used in aural technologies, this time they were used for ophthalmic technologies. Like radars, this technology was also inspired by bats. A bat emits sound waves and listens to the echoes returning back to determine how far away an object is, where it is, how big it is, and where it is moving.

Similarly, project managers and business analysts should be open-minded, find alternative solution options, and prevent shallow "either/or" discussions with business units to be able to resolve conflicts.

Don't Exaggerate Problems

"It is not that I am so smart, it is just that I stay with problems longer." – Albert Einstein.

Sometimes business analysts and project managers feel desperate during requirements gathering meetings when the number of conflicts increases and the problems get complicated. At those times, they should remember that they are not doing rocket science like in NASA or CERN and not exaggerate these situations.

Instead of giving up early, they should remember the advice of Henry Ford: "There are no big problems; there are just a lot of little problems." They should divide problems into smaller parts and resolve them with a bottom-up approach.

As the seniority of business analysts increases, they have a more representative role in their companies. They speak more frequently in front of diverse audiences, and this requires good presentation skills.

Having these skills is also important in convincing business units and developers during negotiations about project issues.

Stage Fright

Presentations, especially in front of a crowd or company executives, are a nightmare for most business analysts. They feel nervous about handling potential problems like unexpected questions or unfriendly attitudes of participants, failing to impress people, or forgetting some of the topics on the slides. In order to feel more comfortable and make better presentations, they can apply the following best practices:

Structure Your Presentation

Presentations should be prepared either with top-down or bottom-up structure. Otherwise, the presenter may have difficulties in describing the scattered topics.

If the presentation is for company executives or business units, it is better to apply a top-down approach that starts with business objectives and moves through solution details.

If the presentation is for technical people, it is better to apply a bottom-up approach that starts with technical details and refers to business objectives when needed.

Use Action Titles

Sometimes the scope of the presentation may be wide and the presenter may not have enough experience or knowledge about the topics. In these situations, using action titles to summarize the topics on each slide will be helpful to remember major points.

Be the Master of Your Presentation

You don't have to go over every slide during your presentation. If you have already provided the intended message during discussions at previous slides, you don't have to present the rest of slides. Otherwise, recurring topics will be boring and even confusing for participants.

Once a salesman visited our office to introduce his company's new generation printers and made this mistake. At the fifth slide of his presentation he managed to convince our team to buy one of his products. However, the salesman continued to present the rest of the slides. After being shown other products, our team decided to change their order to another product. But, the selected product was out of stock and would not be available until six months later. Our team was confused and told the salesman that they needed more time to make a decision. In other words, the salesman missed a done deal by unnecessarily continuing his sales presentation.

Move and Interact

Instead of speaking behind a lectern, the presenter should walk among the audience and interact with them during the presentation. By asking questions and getting comments, the presenter can transform the presentation into a workshop atmosphere and reduce his or her stress level.

During presentations there may be negative people disturbing the presenter with their comments and questions. As a generally accepted principle, the best way to manage stress is to confront it. Hence the presenter should move toward the person who creates anxiety rather than moving away from him or her.

Be Natural

To communicate effectively the expressions (face, gestures, posture) of the presenter should be natural and frank. To apply theatrical expressions (usually taught in courses about presentation techniques) may result in an artificial and exaggerated impression. Also, simultaneously thinking about which expressions to apply makes it harder for the presenter to focus on the topics.

IT is Not a Show Business

Singers use their star aura to impress people not only with their songs but also with their shows. However, business analysis is not a show business. Instead of worrying about impressing people, analysts should focus on presenting topics in the most clear and correct way. In IT business what is presented is always more important than how it is presented.

Ask Why the Conflict Exists

As it is mentioned by Nobel Prize winner Tinbergen, "There is no white or black in the life, there are different tones of grey." Similarly, it is hard to create an exact win-win situation in software development projects. However, it is still the most constructive and effective way of resolving conflicts. The first rule of creating win-win situations is asking why the conflict exists. Then both parties in the negotiation have to leave their personal egos, behave objectively, and be empathic to find the answer to this question and move forward.

Be Careful with "Yes Men"

"Every truth passes through three stages before it is recognized. In the first it is ridiculed, in the second it is opposed, in the third it is regarded as self-evident." - Arthur Schopenhauer.

Analysts should not personalize the negative comments of business units against their proposed solutions. They should get ready to deal with both "Yes Men" and "No Men" from business units.

"Yes Men" are more dangerous than "No Men." They are silent and friendly during requirements gathering meetings but become aggressive and extremely demanding later at user acceptance tests. Although "No Men" are usually regarded as troublemakers, they are more helpful in identifying and resolving conflicts in the early stages of the project. Resolution of these early-detected conflicts prevents costly change requests at later stages.

8. How Can Business Analysts Make More Effective Presentations?

Ask Why the Conflict Exists

As it is mentioned by Nobel Prize winner Tinbergen, "There is no white or black in the life, there are different tones of grey." Similarly, it is hard to create an exact win-win situation in software development projects. However, it is still the most constructive and effective way of resolving conflicts. The first rule of creating win-win situations is asking why the conflict exists. Then both parties in the negotiation have to leave their personal egos, behave objectively, and be empathic to find the answer to this question and move forward.

Be Careful with "Yes Men"

"Every truth passes through three stages before it is recognized. In the first it is ridiculed, in the second it is opposed, in the third it is regarded as self-evident." - Arthur Schopenhauer.

Analysts should not personalize the negative comments of business units against their proposed solutions. They should get ready to deal with both "Yes Men" and "No Men" from business units.

"Yes Men" are more dangerous than "No Men." They are silent and friendly during requirements gathering meetings but become aggressive and extremely demanding later at user acceptance tests. Although "No Men" are usually regarded as troublemakers, they are more helpful in identifying and resolving conflicts in the early stages of the project. Resolution of these early-detected conflicts prevents costly change requests at later stages.

8. How Can Business Analysts Make More Effective Presentations?

Power of Analogies

Analogy is an effective way to communicate a message and convince people. Using them in your presentations makes your ideas easier to understand by the audience.

People usually don't forget analogies, although they forget why you told them. Hence you can also benefit from analogies when you want to provide sticky messages.

9. Which Documents Should Be Prepared for End-to-End Requirements Management?

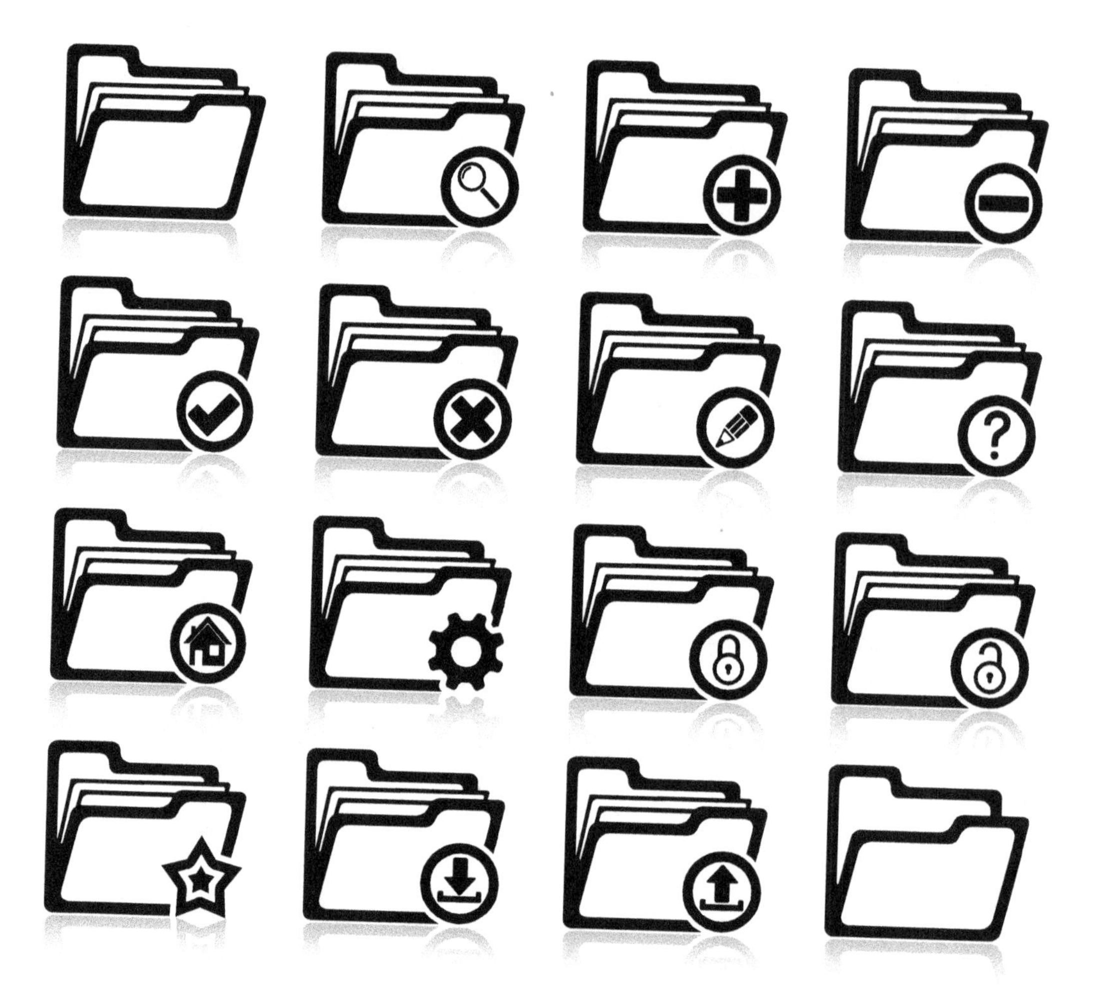

In software development projects, the aim of requirements documents is to provide the answers to these four questions:

- Why: to understand the rationale for the business need and to define the high-level scope of the solution
- What: to define the detailed scope (functional requirements) of the solution
- How: to clarify the quality attributes (non-functional requirements) and business rules of the solution
- Technically How: to depict the inner technical dynamics of the solution

Always Start with Asking the Why Question

Business units' IT requests can be classified under three groups: large-scale projects, medium-/small-sized projects, and enhancement/modification requests. The first question to ask after each business unit request should be why the request is needed.

For large-scale projects that last six months or more, the answers to the Why question should be documented on a business case document as business requirements. For example, business requirements for a CRM (customer relationship management) solution can be defined as generating upsell and cross-sell opportunities, proactively preventing churn, and tracking real-time sales performance.

A clear definition of business requirements is important in the sense that all of the user requirements during the project will be accepted or rejected according to their consistency with these business requirements. The business case document should also include major features of the proposed solution and its benefits, costs, risks, and financial return indicators.

For medium- and small-sized projects that last between one and six months, business requirements should be documented on a vision and scope document. This document should also include the features of the proposed solution that will be delivered in each release.

For enhancement/modification requests that last less than one month, there is no need for a business case or vision and scope document. Most of the time a clear explanation of the business need in a one-page document will be enough to understand the scope of work. These requests may be fulfilled by a more agile approach in collaboration with business units without too much documentation.

Then Ask What and How Questions Respectively

After answering the Why question, the answers for the What and How questions can both be defined on use case documents.

Functional requirements are described as use case scenario steps, and they correspond to the answers of the What question. The business rules and non-functional requirements such as performance, usability, privacy, and security for each use case are documented on the same use case document and give the answers for the How question.

User interface designs are also a part of the How question. Nevertheless, user interface details should not be included in use case documents. It is better to show them separately on user interface prototypes.

For example, on a use case document, a sample functional requirement like "User filters the products according to brand, size, or price by selecting from the drop-down menu located on the top left part of the screen" is not a correct definition. It should be simplified as "User filters the products according to brand, size, or price." The GUI elements like drop-down menus and their location on the interfaces should be described in user interface designs but not in use case scenarios.

Finally, Ask the Technically How Question

The Technically How question aims to identify how the system will handle the defined functional and non-functional requirements and business rules within its internal dynamics. These technical details should not be included in use case documents.

For example, "User filters the products and the system lists the relevant products by running product.XML and product.type query" is not a correct use case definition. Instead these technical system requirements can be documented on a separate document called an SRS (software requirements specification document). SRSs should be bundled with other technical design artifacts like data dictionaries, class diagrams, sequence diagrams, and entity relationship diagrams.

Keep the Documents Updated for the Future

These analysis and design documents should be kept updated even after the project. They should serve as a repository of requirements when needed during future modifications of the systems. This will save a lot of time for the project team responsible for later enhancement/modification work.

10. What Should the Detail Level Be for Requirements Documents?

Outcomes/Outputs

In many IT organizations there is a wrong culture of focusing more on outputs (deliverables) instead of outcomes (value). In software development projects, the objective should not be producing fancy documents and elegant diagrams. Instead, the objective should be producing the software that best meets the business needs by using the most appropriate requirements documents and diagrams as a tool. Here the famous principle applies again: "doing the right thing is always more important than doing the thing right."

There is no general rule about the detail level of requirements documents. The famous quotation of Mark Twain applies here: "All generalizations are false, including this one."

We need requirements documents:

- During the project: To translate business needs into software requirements for developers' best understanding
- After the project: To use as a requirements repository for the enhancements/modifications of IT systems.

The detail level of documents should be aligned according to project needs and conditions to best satisfy the above objectives.

Gold Plating

If the detail level of documents is too low, there is a risk of incomplete requirements definition. In this case developers have to guess about product features. They produce software that misses critical requirements, and this triggers a vicious cycle of CRs (change requests).

And sometimes they code extra features that are not included in requirements documents by thinking that the business will be delighted to see them. This situation is called "Gold Plating." Both CRs and Gold Plating are factors that result in scope creep during the project.

Traffic Lights

In daily life there would be chaos if there were no governing rules. For example, although traffic lights seem to be slowing us, traffic would be locked without them.

For software development projects, requirements documents are like the traffic lights in big cities. If we don't use them, the project starts fast but is locked at some later stage. However, in small cities we don't need to locate traffic lights everywhere. Similarly, in small-scale projects we don't have to use very detailed requirements documents.

Project Internal Dynamics

Location of team members at discrete locations may limit the collaboration between the project stakeholders. The same problem may also be observed in outsourced projects. In these situations, the detail level of documents should be increased to ensure clarity and correctness of requirements.

Documentation Is Not Only for Today

Detailed analysis documents prepared during the project also serve as a requirements repository. This makes the deployment of future enhancements and modifications much easier and faster. The documents should be updated after every change, and changes should be tracked using a versioning system.

11. How Can We Best Benefit from the Use Case Technique?

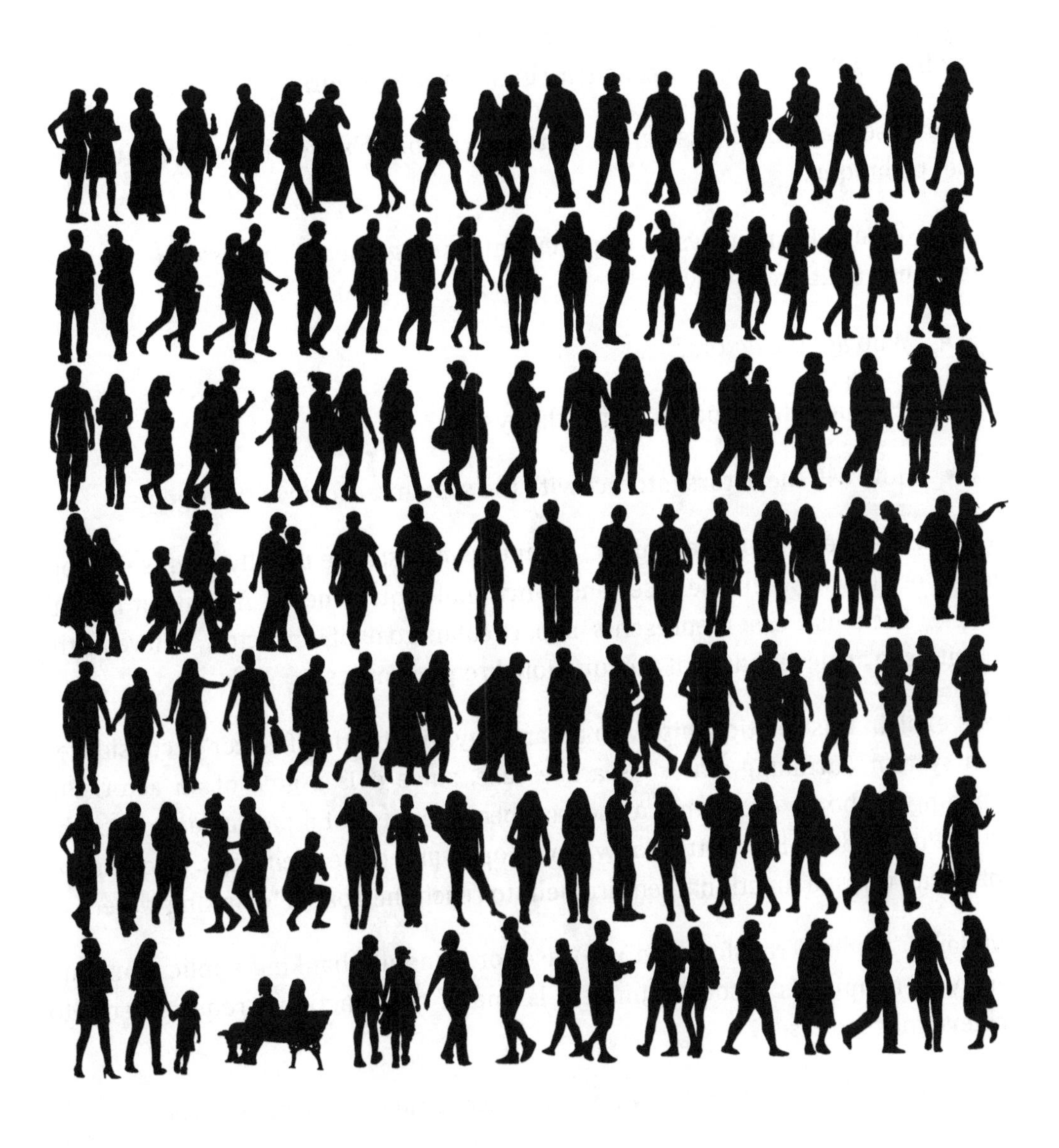

The classical business analysis approach is based on system features. Requirements are gathered by asking the following question:

- Which features should the new system have?

The major drawback of this approach is the huge number of change requests during the project and unused features after the release. The main reason for this drawback is the lack of user centricity in this system-centric approach.

A more user- and business-centric analysis can be achieved by applying the "Use Case" technique.

In use case-driven analysis, requirements are gathered by asking the same question in a different way:

- Who are the actors?
- What are their goals in using the system?
- How will the actors interact with the system to achieve their goals?

When using the use case technique, business analysts are usually confused about the difference between use cases and functional requirements. Actually it is quite simple. Each use case represents a particular goal of an actor, whereas the activities to achieve that goal are functional requirements.

Let's explain this relationship with an analogy: If a bottle of water is considered as a system, "drinking water" is a use case, since it is a goal of an actor. But "opening the bottle cap" is not a use case because it is not a particular goal of the actor. People don't buy bottles of water to open and close their caps. Opening the bottle cap is just a functional requirement to reach the goal of "drinking water."

Similarly "Money Transfer" is a use case for a mobile banking application, and "entry of recipient's account number" is one of the functional requirements to achieve that use case.

In use case definitions, the following best practices should be considered:

- Start with defining a use case diagram depicting each actor and their goals.

  A use case diagram represents the high-level scope of the project.

- Then, prepare a use case document for each use case depicted in the diagram.
- On the document include a brief description; pre-conditions; post-conditions; main, alternative, and exception scenarios; non-functional requirements; business rules; and assumptions of the use case.
- The main scenario represents the positive flow (happy path) of activities to achieve the goal of the actor in normal conditions.

  Alternative scenarios define the other possible ways of achieving the same goal.

  Exception scenarios define the interaction of user and the system in error conditions.

  For the "Money Transfer" use case in a mobile banking application: If sending the money from the deposit account is the main scenario, then the discrete activities needed to send the money from the credit card account can be defined within an alternative scenario. The interaction between the user and the system during the attempts to transfer money from a deposit account with zero balance or after cut-off time can be defined as exception scenarios.
- Define exception scenarios separately from alternative scenarios.

  Because alternative scenarios may include some nice-to-have conditions that can be postponed until future releases in case there is latency in the project.

  However, exception scenarios include error conditions, and they have to be implemented in any case.
- Use cases aim to answer What and How questions.

  Clarifying the Technically How question is not their objective. Hence don't include technical details on use case documents.
- Define use case scenarios with users' point of view.

  However, don't include user interface details on them.

For example, "user selects the deposit account from drop-down menu located on the upper left part of the screen" is a wrong scenario activity definition. "User selects the deposit account" is enough definition. Show user interface details separately on prototypes.

- In use case scenarios define business rules in a parametric way.

  This will let the team easily code, change, and cancel business rules on the system.

  For example, in the "Money Transfer" use case: "User is notified with a message indicating that 5 percent commission will be charged for money transfers after 4:30 p.m." is a wrong scenario activity definition. Instead it should be defined as: "User is notified with a message indicating the commission rate (BR1) that will be charged for money transfers out of allowed time intervals (BR2)." Business rules in this scenario should be defined at the business rules section of the same use case document. The business rules can be defined as:

  BR1: Money Transfer Commission = 5 percent

  BR2: Allowed time intervals for money transfer: 9:00 a.m.–4:30 p.m.

- Define non-functional requirements like usability, performance, and privacy for each use case in a verifiable (testable) way.

  For example, "money transfer should be fast" is not a correct performance requirement definition. It can be defined as "After the request is submitted, money transfer should be completed within two seconds."

- Assumptions are conditions on which the user or system has no control.

  For example, "the accuracy of foreign exchange data received from the central bank" may be an assumption for the "Money Transfer" use case. But, "all users that attempt for a money transfer have a positive account balance" is not a correct assumption. The behavior of the user and the system in the case of an insufficient account balance should be defined as an exception scenario on the use case document.

- Benefit from activity diagrams to simplify use case definitions including complex scenarios.

For software with many internal algorithmic computations but limited user intervention (like embedded software), the use case technique can be impractical and useless to define requirements. Applying a classical system-centric, feature-based analysis approach works better for these kinds of systems.

12. Does Agile Mean No Documentation?

There is one statement in the agile manifesto that differentiates it from other SDLC (systems development life cycle) methodologies, especially from waterfall:

- "Working software over comprehensive documentation"

In Scrum, which is a popular agile framework, requirements are defined as short and simple user stories (As a "role," I want "goal") in parallel with the above manifesto statement.

User stories are defined and prioritized in the product backlog by a business unit representative called the Product Owner. He or she is the voice of the customer. In theoretical formulation there is no need for business analysts or their detailed requirements documents because the product owner and the agile development team (consists of developers and testers) work together at the same location under the coordination of a Scrum Master.

However, in practice there are some difficulties in realizing this theoretical framework.

Business Analysts Are Back

Product owners (with no IT knowledge) have difficulties in speaking the same language with developers (with no business knowledge). This makes it harder to translate business needs into requirements.

Additionally, product owners can rarely spend enough time with the agile team during their own department's busy times, and this makes the situation even harder.

To prevent these problems, business analysts have started to play the product owner role or have been involved in the team that used to be composed of only developers and testers.

Use Case Documents Are Back

In large-scale projects, one-sentence user stories become insufficient for end-to-end definitions of requirements. Lack of scenario-based workflows and missing exception conditions for business rules results in integration problems between the new and already released parts of the software.

These problems bring latencies and quality issues after several iterations and create conflicts between project stakeholders who get used to the fast delivery at initial iterations.

To overcome these challenges, the use case documentation technique has started to also gain acceptance in agile projects.

As a summary, although the more collaborative approach that comes with agile minimizes the need for detailed documentation, it doesn't completely remove it, especially for mid- and large-scale projects.

13. How Can We Prevent Scope Creep Caused by Change Requests?

In each field of software engineering, there are undesirable situations. For developers it is unstable code. For testers it is a bug that can't be reproduced. And for business analysts it is CRs (change requests) of business units.

CRs are disturbing because they:

- can't be planned
- may result in scope creep
- cause analysis paralysis
- generate hidden costs
- are mostly urgent
- are usually sent as defects
- have both direct and indirect impacts on various parts of the system
- may bring a regression testing burden.

There are two main reasons for CRs:

The first one is "changing business needs and market conditions," such as a new regulation, a new product feature in response to competitors, or a major change in technology. This group of CRs usually has the potential to impact the company at the strategic level. Therefore, they should be included in the product scope and implemented. If the change brings a huge impact on the current product scope, the project manager, business analysts, and business unit representatives should come together and work on a new project plan.

The second reason for CRs is the "problems and deficiencies in requirements gathering, documentation, and management process." These kinds of CRs should be prevented in a proactive way by applying the following best practices throughout the project:

Scoping:

- Prepare a business case or vision and scope document in collaboration with the business unit and clearly show the scope of each release.
- Prepare use case diagrams to visualize the solution scope.

Requirements Gathering:

- Don't try to find the answers of Why (we need the solution), What (the system does), How (the system does), and Technically How (the system works) questions at one single meeting.
- Conduct separate sessions for interviews, focus groups, and workshops if your project is not a time-sensitive fast track one.
- In interviews define business requirements and high-level scope with business unit managers.

  In focus groups identify user requirements of a specific business domain.

  In workshops invite representatives from different business domains to ensure consistency while translating user requirements into end-to-end functional requirements, non-functional requirements, and business rules.
- Ensure the alignment of user requirements with business requirements.
- In addition to meetings, conduct field analysis, like job shadowing and user task analysis, to identify user profiles, personas, and their real needs.
- To the meetings, invite not only managers but also people responsible for daily operations.
- Benefit from prototyping during requirements gathering meetings if business unit representatives have difficulty in visualizing requirements in their minds.
- During requirements gathering meetings, be user centric and ask, "What are the user's needs and how will the new system meet them?" instead of asking, "What should be the features of the new system?"
- Don't make assumptions and provide early solutions. First, understand the "AS IS" and then discuss the "TO BE."
- Listen more and talk less during requirements gathering sessions.
- Prepare in advance for the meetings by analyzing the current system's user interfaces and documentation.

- Don't be afraid of conflicts and negotiations. The more conflicts resolved in requirements gathering meetings means fewer CRs during the project.
- Try to clarify all of the issues during the meetings. Don't postpone them by entering them into an issue database.
- Don't be afraid of asking questions when something is not clear.
- Use your IT knowledge to evaluate technical cost and feasibility of business unit requests.
- Invite developers to the meetings to clarify the issues about technical constraints.

Requirements Documentation:

- Don't include technical details in requirements documents that are sent to business units.
- Don't list the answers of Why, What, How, and Technically How questions in the same document.

  List business requirements (answers of why) on business case or vision and scope documents; functional requirements (answers of what) and non-functional requirements and business rules (answers of how) on use case documents; and technical system requirements (answers of technically how) on software requirements specification (SRS) documents.
- Differentiate must-have and nice-to-have requirements by prioritizing them.
- Define requirements in a clear and testable format.
- Define business rules in a parametric way.
- Check the consistency of requirements listed on different analysis documents.

Sign-off Process:

- Organize formal review meetings with developers to evaluate the technical feasibility of requirements before sending them for sign-off to the business units.

  Remember that people don't forget what is promised to them.

- Don't trust e-mail approvals from business units during the sign-off process.

  For large-scale projects, print the requirements documents and request signatures of business unit representatives.

Static Testing and Reviews:

- Ensure that requirements documents are reviewed by experienced business analysts before they are sent for business unit sign-off.
- Include requirements reviews within the software testing team's static testing efforts.
- Ensure that the testing team starts preparing test cases after requirements are baselined with business unit sign-off.

CR Management Process:

- Implement a change control process that is not bureaucratic.
- Use a traceability matrix to evaluate the impact of each CR.
- Evaluate CRs by considering their business value and technical cost rather than the requester business unit's political power in the company.

14. How Can Automation Help Us in Requirements Management?

In recent years, we have started to see a different "ware" category like hard-ware and soft-ware. This category is called "shelf-ware." Shelf-ware represents the automation software that sits on the shelves of the company without being used by any single person.

Shelf-ware causes a huge amount of sunk cost for IT departments. In some public companies, high license and support costs paid for useless software has become an issue investigated during internal audits.

To prevent the shelf-ware situation, the following best practices should be taken into consideration during automation of the requirements management process:

Tools Are Wizards, but Not Magicians

Some IT managers want to press a button and let the computer automatically do the majority of analysis, design, and testing work instead of utilizing people for these tasks. Unfortunately, this is only a management dream.

Tools are wizards, but not magicians. They have limits. They can only help the project team do their work in a more convenient way by automating some of their tasks, but not all of them.

Think Big but Start Small

If the IT organization's process maturity is at a good level, automation makes it better; otherwise, automation may even make it worse. Hence IT managers should first focus on improving their team's requirements management skills and then give the start for the automation initiative.

If the team has no knowledge on basic techniques like use cases, traceability matrices, impact analysis, black box test techniques, and low fidelity prototyping, then automation will only bring extra problems rather than benefits and will accelerate the chaos.

An iterative approach of first implementing these techniques by using simple templates and then adapting the automation tools is the best-proven way of success.

Adam Smith and Software Engineering

Like the manufacturing industry, Adam Smith's division of labor theory has also gained acceptance in software engineering. By using the new SDLC (systems development life cycle) tools, demand management, project management, business analysis, user interface design, technical design, coding, and testing processes can be managed in integration with each other on a common platform.

Requirements management tools let you receive, prioritize, and plan requests from business units.

Then they guide you in preparation of analysis documents. The requirements defined on these documents are automatically stored in a repository to enable end-to-end traceability.

Analysis and design diagrams like activity diagrams, sequence diagrams, and class diagrams can be prepared on these tools. With their integration with IDEs like Eclipse, they can automatically generate code by using the details on the design diagrams.

Test cases can be easily prepared by importing the requirements from the analysis module and combining them with risk-based test conditions. Regression tests can be automated by creating capture-and-play, data-driven, or keyword-driven test scripts on these tools. The defects found after each test run can then be associated with the relevant test cases, requirements, and projects.

In parallel to these activities, every update on the code, analysis, design, and test artifacts can be tracked by configuration management capability.

Application Lifecycle Management

Although these SDLC tools provide an integrated end-to-end requirements management capability, they have limitations in providing a collaborative platform for the project team.

New generation tools called ALM (Application Lifecycle Management) have gained popularity by filling this gap with a Facebook-like architecture. On these tools project team members at discrete locations can work in the same virtual workplace. In this virtual workplace, project team members are represented virtually, and their work is published as status updates. They can work together on the same project documents and user interface prototypes. They are notified for every change on requirements, code, and test artifacts by advanced configuration management features.

This virtual collaboration makes the usage of agile methodologies like Scrum possible even for distributed teams at discrete locations.

People Look at the Score, Not How One Played During the Game

Automation is a challenging project itself. Project managers should consider the time needed to implement automation tools as a separate risk item in every project. They should not use an automation tool for the first time in a time-sensitive high-priority project. The team should focus on the project itself, instead of allocating their limited time for tool implementation. Project managers should remember that upper management always takes account the score, but not how the team played during the game.

15. What Is the Best Way of Benefiting from UML in Software Analysis and Design?

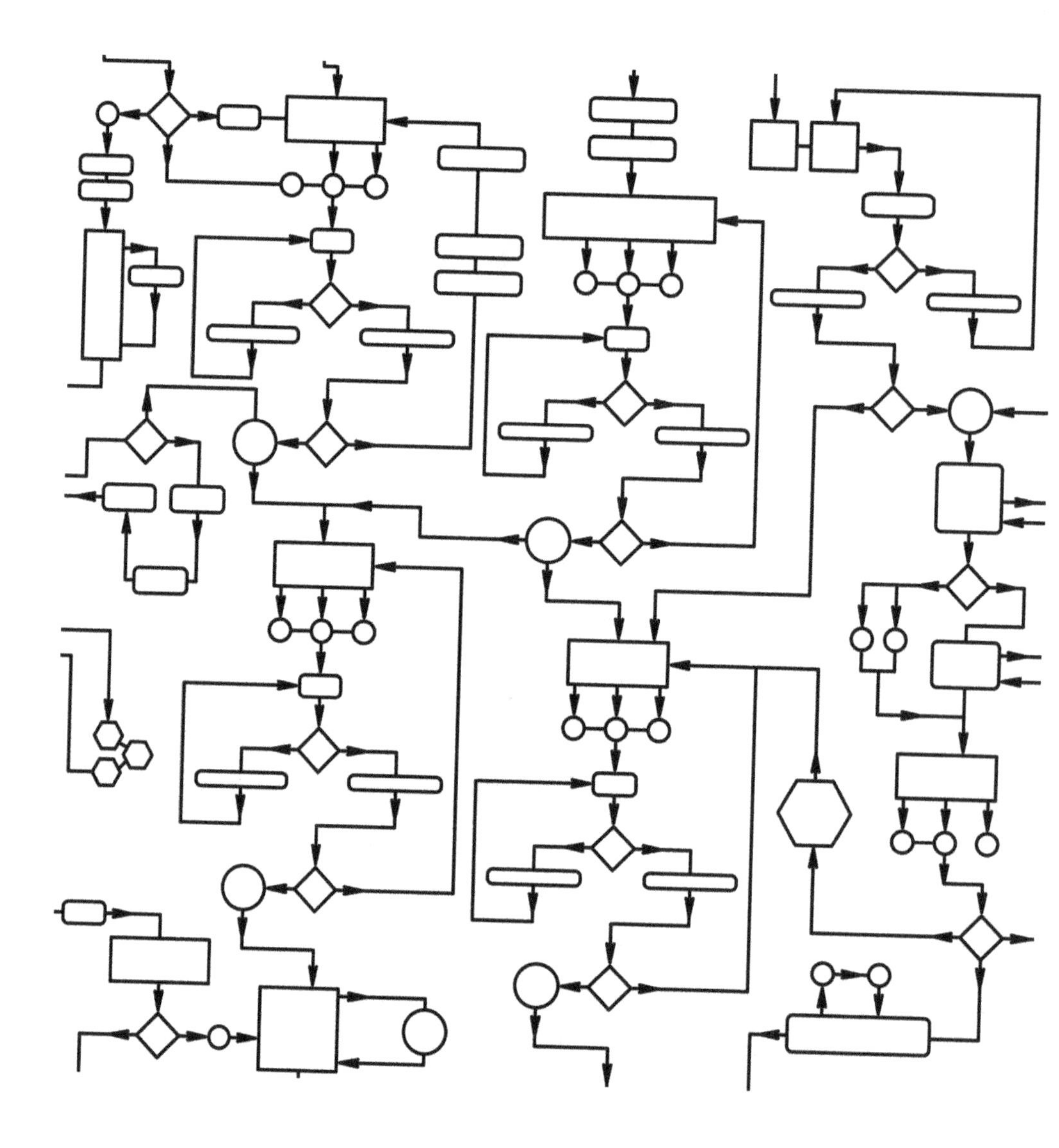

Software modeling is similar to mathematical modeling of physics laws. Software is like the universe: requirements and business rules are the laws of physics and modeling diagrams are the mathematical models to describe them.

Newton vs. Quantum Models

Mathematical techniques in calculus like derivatives and integrals were formulated by Isaac Newton to model laws of physics. He invented them as tools to prove his theories about the laws of physics. However, after verification of Heisenberg's Quantum models, it was realized that Newton's mathematical models were not able to make accurate calculations for atomic particles moving at velocities close to the speed of light. Nevertheless, engineers still continue to use Newton models rather than complicated Quantum models in the engineering of daily life objects.

Similarly, UML (Unified Modeling Language) was formulated as a technique to define software requirements in a more structured way. In most projects drawing some of the basic UML diagrams is more than enough to define requirements instead of modeling the software in full detail. UML should be used as a pragmatic modeling technique rather than a set of complex project deliverables.

Drawings vs. Letters

In history, people first used drawings in their communications with each other. Even after the invention of letters, they continued to use drawings as an easy way of expressing themselves.

Similarly, using UML diagrams is an effective way of improving communication between analysts and other project stakeholders. Use case and activity diagrams are very helpful for business analysts in communicating user requirements to business units. On the other hand, class diagrams and sequence diagrams are very helpful to system analysts in communicating software design details to developers. These diagrams help clarify the ambiguities in narrative requirements definitions on plain-text analysis documents.

Discovery of Neptune

According to famous physician Stephen Hawking, a model is good fit if it is "elegant, contains few arbitrary elements, agrees with observations, and makes future predictions." An example to his assertion is Neptune, which is the first planet that was discovered by using mathematical formulations. By modeling the gravitational forces on the orbit of the Uranus planet, Neptune's mass and exact location was calculated. These findings were later verified by telescopic observations.

UML should serve the modeling of software architecture in a similar manner. Software should be modeled in a simple, clear, extendable, and parametric structure. In order to achieve this, business analysts should learn the logic of UML rather than memorizing its notations.

UML Is Not Applicable for Every Type of Project

Using UML is not appropriate for every type of project. In data-driven projects like data warehousing, data mining, or OLAP reporting, it is better to use structural modeling techniques including data-flow and entity relationship diagrams. And for modeling workflow applications, it is more practical to use simple flowcharts instead of UML diagrams.

16. Which Methodology Is the Best Fit for Your Project: Waterfall or Agile?

Since "agile" has a similar meaning to "quick," which is the most nice-to-hear word in the IT business, it became popular in a very short time.

Dialectics

According to the Dialectical method in philosophy, "within themselves all things contain internal dialectical contradictions that are the primary cause of motion, change, and development in the world."

Similarly, the internal contradictions and drawbacks of the waterfall methodology have been the driving force behind agile adoption. The most crucial of these drawbacks is lack of early product delivery at waterfall projects. Since coding waits for the completion of analysis and design phases, in a one-year project it takes at least five to six months on average to start getting the working parts of the software. This latency in delivery creates anxiety on business units who are impatient to see "quick" results. On the other hand, agile projects' fast delivery of working software starting from the first iteration brings confidence to all stakeholders.

The second major drawback of waterfall is its low flexibility against changes to requirements. Any possible change to the requirements has an impact on the overall analysis and design artifacts. In agile environments a change to the requirements has no effect on the parts of the software that have not been analyzed yet.

However, resolution of waterfall's drawbacks by agile remains "too good to be true" unless the following best practices are adapted:

Agile or Waterfall?

Applying agile methodology to every kind of project is not a correct strategy. It is still more appropriate to proceed with waterfall, especially for the development of software that has intensive integration among its components. If agile is applied to these kinds of projects, the following happens: The team delivers software parts A and B without any major problems at the first iterations. Nevertheless, the team realizes that they have to make changes to parts A and B while working on part C since it has integration points with those parts. In other words, A and B have to be refactored although they have already been released. Refactoring means changing an existing code without changing its behavior, and it is always harder than coding from scratch. These back-and-forth moves with challenging refactoring efforts make the build and delivery of the integrated software even more difficult at later iterations, making waterfall a better alternative.

Another difficulty in applying agile methodology is faced when project team members are at discrete locations. The backbone of the agile manifesto is "customer collaboration over contract negotiation." This condition is usually hard to maintain in most companies because business analysts, developers, testers, and business units usually work at different locations on more than one project at the same time. The only way to bring these people together is having them meet at the same virtual environment provided by new generation ALM (Application Lifecycle Management) tools. But these tools can't fully provide the comfort, efficiency, and effectiveness of being in the same physical environment.

Although it is not appropriate to apply agile to every project, it is still possible to benefit from its manifesto in waterfall projects by doing the following:

- Applying a time-boxing approach for better release planning,
- Conducting periodical retrospective meetings to discuss lessons learned,
- Benefiting from prototyping to get early feedback from the users in a more iterative way, and
- Increasing the number of formal requirements review meetings to increase collaboration between project stakeholders.

17. Do We Still Need Business Analysts and Project Managers in Agile Projects?

Business analyst and project management communities started to get worried after the agile methodologies like Scrum started to gain popularity because their roles were missing in this new way of software development. They were basically replaced by the product owner and Scrum master roles.

Scrum Master vs. Project Manager

The Scrum master is responsible for managing each iteration's kickoff, planning, monitoring, execution and closure activities. These tasks are similar to the five process areas that are already applied by project managers to every project. Except for a couple of new techniques like sprint meetings, time-boxing, burn-down charts, and retrospectives, the most major change is the title of the role. Hence Scrum masters are usually selected from project managers in IT organizations.

Product Owner vs. Business Analyst

But, for business analysts the situation is more complicated. They are totally replaced by a new role called the product owner, who is usually selected from the business units. The product owner is responsible for defining the requirements in user story format and prioritizing them in a repository called the product backlog. However, this theoretical formulation of the product owner role usually fails in practice due to various reasons.

First of all, a product owner should have a good level of business knowledge and experience in order to make correct and complete requirements definitions. However, in most companies, business unit managers prefer to assign junior people to IT projects as product owners. They keep the experienced people for the critical business activities of their own departments. In addition to experience, junior business representatives also lack requirements elicitation and management skills. This brings extra risk to the success of the product owner role, which is the most crucial role in Scrum.

Another risk of assigning people from business units to the product owner role is their lack of IT knowledge, which results in communication problems with developers throughout the project. IT knowledge is also needed to prioritize requirements, change requests, and defects. The technical constraints and difficulties mentioned by developers should be understood and assessed together with the business impact of these work items. Business analysts are the only people in most companies who have both business and technical knowledge that is needed to make these assessments.

User Stories vs. Use Cases

Another challenge of product owners is related to documentation of requirements. Although minimum documentation is an important aspect of the agile manifesto, sometimes it is very challenging to fulfill the requirements documentation needs with one-sentence user stories. Especially in mid- and large-scale projects with many integration points and intense user interactions, user stories have to be replaced by use case documentation. Although the use case definition is a simple and usable technique for business analysts, it is complicated for people from business units who have no or limited knowledge of requirements analysis techniques.

To overcome these challenges, an experienced business analyst should be assigned to the product owner role instead of a person from the business units. In case the product owner is still selected from business units, the agile team should not only include developers and testers but also business analysts.

18. What Is the Impact of Agile on Software Testers?

In agile projects the project team should ensure that the system continues its operation without any failure after the deployment of new components at each iteration.

Changing the Tire of a Moving Car

Adding components to a live system without impacting the released parts is like changing the tire of a car while it's moving.

This iterative development approach requires comprehensive regression testing of the system components released at previous iterations. To ensure enough test coverage, the parts with both direct and indirect integration points should be retested. This brings a huge amount of extra testing effort. Testing the same components manually and repetitively is both time-consuming and impractical.

To make this process more efficient, automated regression test suites should be created. Normally it is possible to benefit from capture and play test automation tools in stable development environments.

However, it is very difficult to use these tools in agile projects, since the software is continuously changed in a very dynamic development environment. The continuous changes to system components make the prerecorded test scripts useless.

To ensure maintainability, API-level test scripts should be created instead of GUI-based scripts generated on capture and play tools. This requires a technical test team with advanced coding skills.

I Am Not a Tester!

Usually it is very hard to find these kinds of technical testers. In this case developers are made responsible to code test automation scripts. But after a while, they start to complain that they are developers not testers.

This issue should be planned as a risk item during resource planning of each agile project.

Lack of Test Basis

In mid- and large-scale software development projects, testers need to prepare comprehensive test cases. To ensure enough coverage, they should form the test basis according to requirements details and combine them with test conditions based on business rules and risk-based exception scenarios.

In waterfall projects use case documents include all of these details and can be used as a good test basis. However, in agile projects, simple user story definitions and high-level acceptance criteria miss the required details to create comprehensive test cases.

To ensure enough coverage, testers in agile projects should have more business knowledge compared to testers in waterfall projects.

19. What Is User-Centered Interface Design?

If your objective is to design the best user interface, it is not a good starting point. Instead you should change your point of view and focus on creating the best UX (user experience).

User-Centered Analysis and Design

The best user experience can be achieved by applying a user-centered analysis and design approach in which user interfaces are driven by users' goals and profiles.

In this approach business analysts define user profiles in addition to user requirements during elicitation sessions.

An effective way to understand user profiles is by asking users their opinions about the current system. Users' comments about the system can be interpreted to understand their own capabilities and weaknesses. This reminds us of one of the quotations of famous philosopher Spinoza: "If Pierre tells something about Paul, we learn more about Pierre than we learn about Paul."

After gathering the requirements and definitions of user profiles, the use case technique can be used to document requirements.

In this technique first the actors (users) and their goals (use cases) are determined. Then, the interactions of actors with the system to meet their goals are defined. Finally, these interactions are grouped to form user interfaces on low-fidelity prototyping tools by also considering the characteristics of each user profile.

This user-centered approach ensures both functionality and usability.

UX Teams

In cases where requirements documents are directly sent to visual designers without any prototypes, designers have difficulty understanding these documents before designing the user interfaces.

Although the interfaces they create are elegant, they usually have usability and functionality problems. Companies that want to mitigate this risk establish dedicated UX teams.

UX specialists work on the low-fidelity prototypes created by business analysts and improve their usability by applying UX design principles. They also conduct usability tests with real users to find and fix the usability problems on the prototypes.

Afterward they send the prototypes to visual designers. By working this way, visual designers spend their limited time creating the most aesthetic visual designs instead of struggling to understand analysis documents.

However, in small-scale companies there may be no budget for a separate UX team, and their role may have to be played by business analysts. Business analysts working in these organizations should spend more time and effort improving their knowledge of UX design principles and usability testing techniques.

20. What Is the Gaudi Way of User Interface Design?

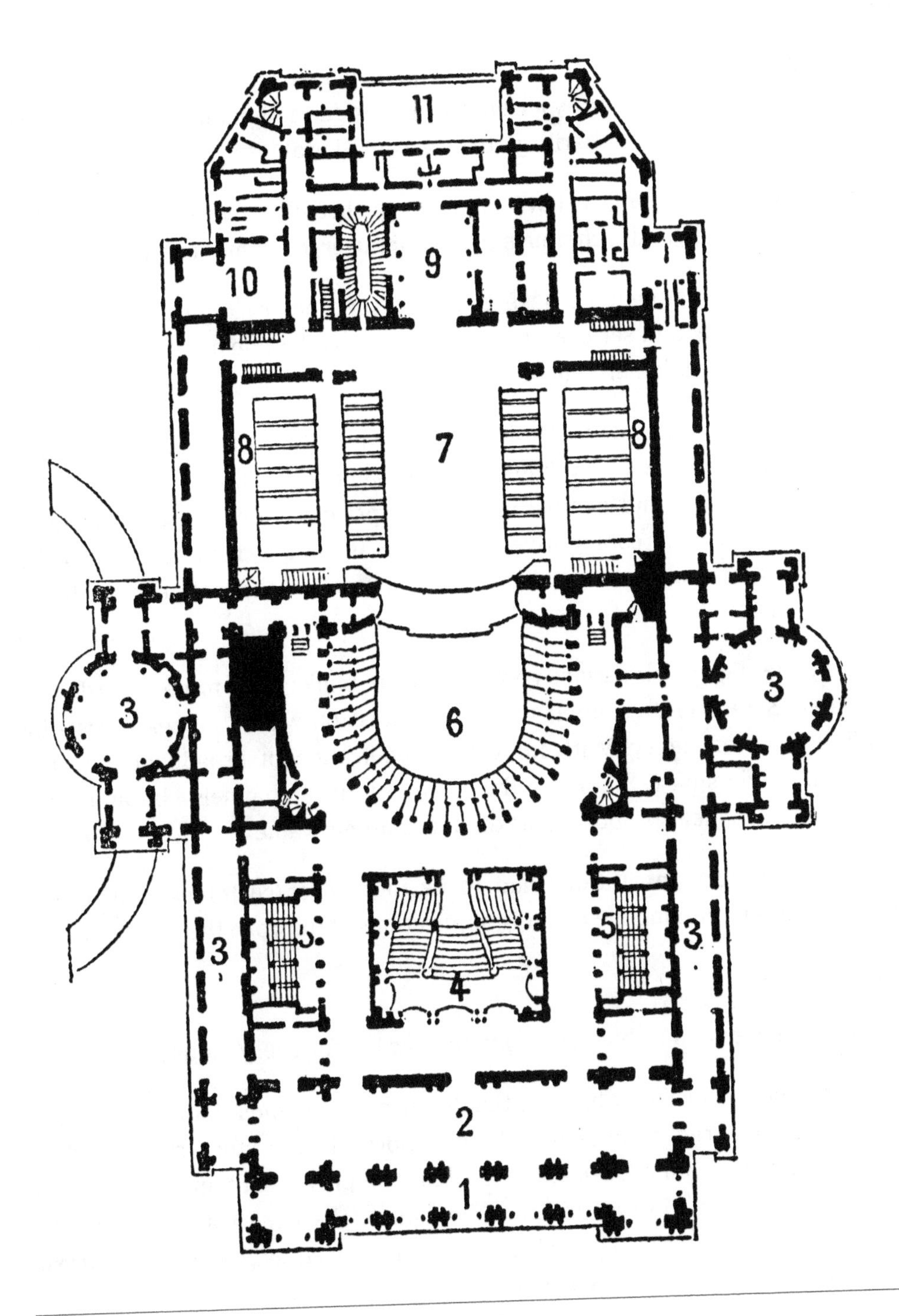

User interface design is like football. Everybody in the company feels confident and keen to comment on the designs. Upper management also loves to intervene in the design process by requesting last-minute changes even on colors and page layouts on the eve of the product release.

Overcoming this challenge and designing user interfaces in a professional environment requires a user experience (UX) design methodology that positions the user at the center and inherits globally accepted usability principles.

In recent years companies have started to heavily invest in UX design methodologies, tools, and techniques to be more user/customer centric.

This is a right investment because today competitors can quickly copy your company's products and services, but it takes a considerable amount of time for them to copy your customer-centric approach.

Financial services is one of the industries in which this situation can be best observed. Today almost every bank has the same portfolio of commoditized products and services. And, competing with low price is not sustainable for them. The only way to gain competitive advantage is to be customer centric by providing the best experience on all customer interaction channels, especially the self-service ones.

Previously the digital self-service channels of the banks used to be regarded as "alternative" self-service channels whose only mission was to decrease costs by providing more efficiency. With increased penetration of broadband Internet connection and smart phones, these alternative channels became the "mainstream" channels, proposing maximum customer value.

As a result, financial institutions had to be more user/customer centric and redesign their web and mobile banking applications to improve their usability.

Organic Design

This evolution has been viable not only in finance but for every industry.

Throughout the construction history, Gaudi has been the most famous architect with his user-centered architecture design approach. His story starts with a childhood suffering from poor health. This situation prevented him from going to school, and he spent most of his time in nature. His observations of nature inspired his design approach, which can be summarized as follows: "The great book always open and which we should make an effort to read, is that of Nature."

With this philosophy he designed buildings with "organic style," which then became an important standard in architecture.

Natural-Born Users

Another man revolutionized the high-tech industry in a similar way. By positioning users at the center of the analysis and design process, Steve Jobs led the innovation of the most usable consumer electronics products ever.

He achieved to create natural-born users of his products. Even kids can use his company's phones and touchpads with gestures similar to their natural behavior. This new design approach made his company the best performer in the high-tech industry.

After the success of this approach, it was realized that the humanization of software is not necessarily achieved by anthropomorphic features but mainly by ensuring usability.

User Profiling

In user interface design, the first step to adapt Gaudi's and Steve Jobs's ways of user centricity is user profiling.

User profiling involves grouping users according to their level of potential computer use (which depends on characteristics like age, gender, education, and business background) and then designing user interfaces in alignment to these user profiles.

Personas and Emotional Design

Another important aspect of user centricity is emotional design. Human beings judge something according to their left brain logic and right brain emotion. And most of the time, emotion is the main criteria in their judgments.

In alignment with their emotions, users first create a mental model of the products they use. This model guides them throughout their whole experience with the product. User interface designs should be based on users' mental model rather than designers'.

Personas, which are representative imaginary characters, are the best way to define the mental models of diverse user profiles and predict their expected behavior on user interfaces.

In summary, user centricity is a “must-have” rather than a “nice-to-have” in interface design.

However, it does not mean doing everything according to users’ wants. Designers should focus on defining profiles, creating personas, and understanding mental models to identify users’ real needs and capabilities, but at the same time they should be innovative during the design process. This fact is best summarized in Henry Ford’s famous quotation: "If I had asked people what they wanted, they would have said faster horses."

21. Why Is Simple Difficult in User Interface Design?

$$y'_u \quad y = u^2 + 3\sqrt{u} - 1 \quad u = x^4 + 1 \quad y'_x =$$

$$' = (u^2 + 3\sqrt{u} - 1)'_u (x^4 + 1)'_x = (2u + \frac{3}{2\sqrt{u}})*4x \quad y'_x = (2x^4 + 2 + \frac{3}{2\sqrt{x^4 - 1}})*4x =$$

$$\lim_{x \to \infty} (1 + \frac{2}{x})^{x+5} = ((1 + \frac{2}{x})^{\frac{x}{2}})^2 * (1 + \frac{2}{x})^5 \quad \lim_{x \to}$$

$$e^2 * 1 = e^2 \quad \lim_{x \to a} \sqrt[p]{f(x)} = \sqrt[p]{\lim_{x \to a} f(x)}$$

$$A \lim b^{f(x)} = b^A, \quad b = const, \quad \lim_{x \to a} f(x) =$$

$$\lim_{x \to a} \log_c f(x) = \log_c [\lim f(x)], \quad c = const \quad \lim_{x \to}$$

Instead of searching for the best style sheets and design patterns, companies should first focus on adapting UX (user experience) design principles in their user interface design process.

Once adapted, these principles that are based on human behavior assure the usability of interfaces designed in the company. One of the most important UX principles is simplicity.

Simple Is Difficult

The best user interfaces are simplistic and intuitive ones in which users can easily find what they are looking for and complete their tasks with minimum effort and error.

On the opposite side, busy and noisy interfaces make the experience complicated for users. These kinds of designs can be easily created by distributing the functional specs randomly on different parts of the interface without too much design thinking.

However, it is not that easy to create simplistic and intuitive designs. These designs require extra time and effort. The secret to achieve simplicity in design is best explained in the quotation from famous novelist Antoine de Saint Exupery: "A designer knows he has achieved perfection not when there is nothing left to add, but when there is nothing left to take away."

In simplifying user interfaces, Einstein's quotation should also be remembered to prevent the risk of false simplicity: "Everything should be made as simple as possible, but not simpler." The unnecessary parts of the interface should be removed to make the interface simpler unless these parts clear away the functionality of the system.

This simplistic approach is also valid in the preparation of user interface content. The content should be expressed with a minimum number of words. Mark Twain's quotation describes this situation very well: "I didn't have time to write a short letter, so I wrote a long one instead." This simplistic approach has also been the differentiating success factor for Twitter in replacing classical blog sites.

Balance "Easy to Use" and "Easy To Learn"

Ideally user interfaces should be designed simple enough to leave no need for learning how to use the system.

Nevertheless, this is sometimes challenging, especially for transaction-intensive software used for internal company operations. In spite all of the efforts, it may be hard to simplify the interfaces of these systems.

If they are not "easy to use" then they should be "easy to learn." This can be achieved by designing interfaces in a consistent way. Consistency lets employees apply the knowledge they have gained while using one part of the software during their experience with the other parts. In case employees still have questions, the system can guide them with contextual help menus and user manuals.

Also, there is the possibility of training employees about how to use the software. Through training shortcomings about "easiness to use" can be compensated by "easiness to learn."

But, it is not feasible to train all customers about how to use the software. Thus, customer-facing company software should always have top-level usability.

22. Which UX Principles Should Be Applied in User Interface Design?

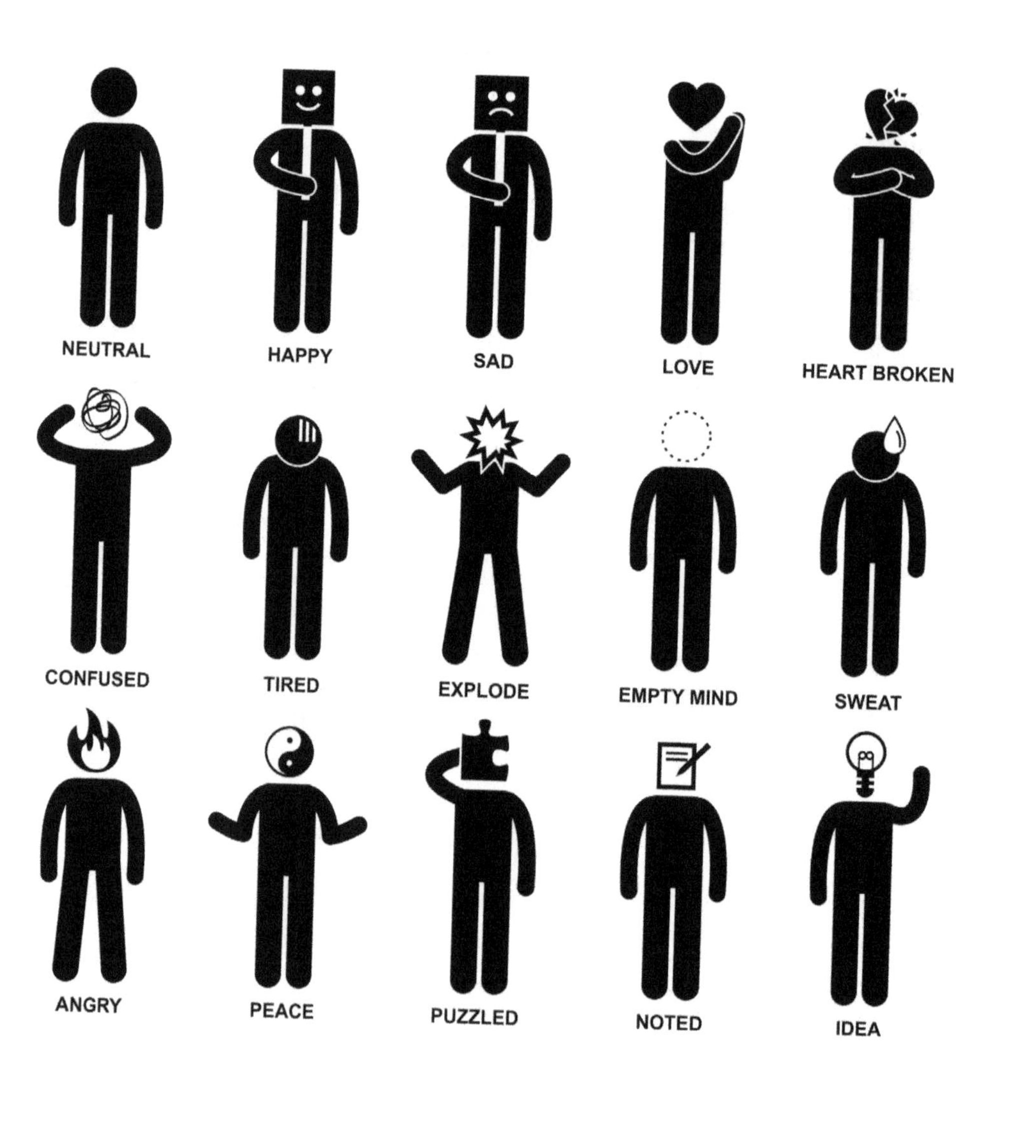

User experience design is a multidisciplinary field based on human computer interaction, computer science, ergonomics, and especially psychology. The following psychological principles should be applied to provide the best experience in user interfaces:

People Have Selective Concentration

People have difficulty focusing on more than one object at the same time. During usability tests with the eye-tracking technique this fact is very apparent. When an informative carousel image is displayed on the upper middle part of the interface, most users at least shoot a glance at it. However, when another image is located next to it, most users ignore both images and don't look at either one.

This fact necessitates selecting the highest priority content and design objects instead of displaying all of them at the same time.

People Expect Consistency

Today most companies provide a ubiquitous computing feature that allows users to start their experience in one interaction channel and complete it in another one.

For example, users booking a flight on a mobile application can buy the ticket on the web page and check in at a kiosk. People expect consistent menu structures, navigation flows, and call-to-actions on all of these interaction channels. Once they complete a transaction successfully at one channel, they expect to complete other transactions the same way on the other channels.

For example, if they once made a credit card payment under the "Credit Cards" menu of the ATM, they expect to also do it under the same menu item on mobile or web channels. If the payment option is placed under another menu, such as "Payments," they have difficulty navigating to the right place.

Baby Duck Syndrome

Baby Duck Syndrome describes the bias of users to evaluate new designs according to their similarity with the old design and usually their preference of the old one.

In usability tests when the users are asked to comment on the new design they usually say, "The older one was better; I don't know why, but it was better!" Due to the Baby Duck Syndrome, it is not wise to change the user interface design too frequently if not really needed.

People Usually Don't Know What You Know

Designers should not assume that users also know everything that they know and think the same way as they do.

For example, in most web-based applications, the only way to navigate back to the home page is by clicking on the logo of the brand. However, in usability tests we see that the majority of novice users don't know this call-to-action. Therefore, another option should be provided for users to navigate back to the home page.

Similarly, in recent mobile applications there is a popular feature called "Send to Cloud" that enables online saving of files to remote servers. In our usability tests, we observe that most novice users don't understand the meaning of cloud in this context and don't use that feature. Interfaces should always speak the language of users and not the designers.

People Prefer Pictures to Text

People first started to draw pictures to communicate with each other before they invented the letters. Today diagrams and pictures are utilized in describing complex issues. Even Einstein said, "If I can't picture it, I can't understand it."

Metaphors are visual figures that resemble an object or activity in real life.

Using metaphors on interface designs is a very effective way of communicating the intended message. To improve usability, self-explanatory metaphors should be used. If users have difficulty in understanding the metaphor, then the metaphor should be used together with a title or brief description explaining what it represents.

Metaphors should also be kept simple. Users should not interpret extra meanings other than the metaphor's purpose of use.

People Group Items

People have a tendency to group items.

According to Gestalt Principles, users form a natural grouping of items according to their attributes like proximity, symmetry, and similarity with each other. To achieve intuitive designs, Gestalt Principles should be applied for appropriate placement of design objects on user interfaces.

People Behave Differently in Different Contexts

Context is one of the most important factors that impacts human behavior in usage of products.

"Context" is usually confused with "content," but they are completely different concepts. Context's explanation in design is very similar to its meaning in archeology. For an archaeologist, context means the place where an artifact is found. The artifact itself (content) is not explanatory enough to make predictions about history. It should be evaluated together with the attributes of the place it is found.

Likewise, context in user interface design refers to the surrounding factors that influence the behavior and expectations of users.

This situation can be easily observed at companies like banks where there are many alternative touch points with customers. User behavior is different at each channel due to contextual factors. For example, while a live video chat feature is a good customer service solution for Internet banking users, it is not a good feature for ATM users due to the negative reactions of impatient customers waiting in the queue.

23. Is Prototyping an Art or Craftsman Work?

Are You a Craftsman or an Artist?

Until the Renaissance, the majority of architects designed their artifacts with a craftsman approach. Aesthetics was still very important for architects, but their main concern was designing buildings, bridges, and fountains that best met the needs of the public.

After the freedom and creativity impact of the Renaissance, architects started to behave more like artists and focused on designing more aesthetic pieces.

Sometimes business analysts get confused whether to behave like artists or like craftsmen during user interface design. Instead of trying to create Picasso—perfect designs with an artistic approach—business analysts should always behave like craftsmen who give focus to meeting the functional needs of business units in the most usable way, leaving aesthetics concerns to designers.

Power of Iterations

Even the most experienced craftsmen can't produce the optimum design at the first trial. Good design is a result of several iterations. Iteration is a cycle of doing something, testing it, improving it, and retesting it. The most efficient way of iterative design is prototyping. This is also valid for user interface design.

Making iterations on the software is a very costly approach, because for every iteration, the code, database, and other technical components of the system have to be changed and retested, whereas changing the prototypes is much easier and faster.

Interactive Prototyping Tools

Recent prototyping tools allow mocking up the software with wireframes by using a rich widget library.

Prototyping tools have features that allow interactive user actions like navigating between pages, selecting options by clicking on radio buttons, and getting notifications by error messages. Thanks to these interactive features, both functionality- and usability-related defects can be found and fixed at the early stages of the project. Since the software is not coded yet, change requests are not painful and costly as they would be at later stages.

Tool selection is an important success factor in prototyping. Despite their wide use, visual design tools are not suitable for prototyping. Since the aim of these design tools is drawing visual objects, business analysts shift their priority from functional and usability aspects to visual details like colors and font types. But, polishing user interfaces is the responsibility of visual designers rather than business analysts.

Prototyping Has Its Own Risks

Prototyping has its own risks.

One of these risks concerns business units. Business units think that software is composed of only interfaces. They usually have no idea about code, database, web server, and other technical components of the software. The first time they see the interactive prototypes they think that the system is ready for release. When they hear that the prototype is only a mock-up and the release will be five months later, they feel disappointed. They accuse business analysts and the project manager of delaying them unnecessarily by not delivering a system that is ready to go live.

To mitigate this risk, business analysts should inform business units in advance about the purpose and scope of the prototyping process.

The other risk in the prototyping process concerns developers. Developers usually don't like to read analysis documents. They prefer to start coding just after they get the preliminary versions of prototypes.

Project managers should prevent this situation and ensure that the coding process waits until the requirements documents are signed off on by business units. Otherwise, it is hard to keep the code updated with changes on requirements documents and user interfaces.

24. What Is the Most Effective Way of Testing Software Usability?

Usability is one of the non-functional requirements like performance, privacy, and reliability that highly impact the quality of software.

It is an indicator of how easy a product can be used by its users.

Like other non-functional requirements, usability of software should be tested in every project before it is released. Project managers should not disregard usability testing efforts in their project plans.

Usability Testing Is Not Expensive

Sometimes project managers hesitate to allocate specific time and budget for usability testing because they think a fully equipped test laboratory is needed to run these tests.

However, rather than being a "must-have," usability labs are a "nice-to-have" facility. Even inviting users to the project room and observing their interaction with the user interfaces and recording their reactions, confusions, errors, and difficulties will be enough to detect and analyze most usability problems.

Test Early

Unlike other testing types, it is possible to test the usability of software that has not been coded yet.

Interactive wireframes built on prototyping tools can be used for usability tests. This allows early detection and fixation of usability defects.

Test with Real Users

Testing usability with a limited number of users who represent target user profiles is much better than testing with a lot of random users.

The optimum number of users that should be included in the tests is eight to ten people for each user profile. For example, to test the usability of an e-commerce application with three different user profiles, inviting a total of thirty people will be more than enough.

Finding users who represent the target user profiles is one of the most challenging parts of usability studies.

The customer database of the company should be queried in an intelligent way to match customers with correct user groups. The selected people should be phone interviewed to check their conformance to target user profiles.

Eyes Don't Lie

Selected users evaluate their experience on the interfaces either by thinking aloud during the test or by answering survey questions after the test session.

In either case the majority of users can't give complete, clear, and objective feedback needed to understand the level of usability. Some of the users don't want to criticize the product and hesitate to make negative comments.

To overcome this situation, a complementary test technique called Eye Tracking can be utilized.

This technique makes it possible to detect the parts of user interfaces where users look while conducting the given tasks. This is done by tracking and recording their eye movements with special equipment and software. Detailed reports like heat maps and gaze plots can be generated by the eye tracking tool.

Although these reports don't tell what the user thought during his or her experience, the reports do make it possible to see where users focused most, in which order they looked at each part of the interface, and how long they stared at each part while completing the tasks.

Eye tracking results should be combined with think-aloud and retrospective evaluations to understand the real user experience and identify usability problems.

Don't Copy Your Competitors' Mistakes

Benchmarking the new design with competitors' user interfaces and making comparisons is an alternative way of evaluating potential UX design and usability issues.

However, even the best competitors don't always do the right things. Benchmarking should not mean copying the mistakes of competitors. Instead of benchmarking results, the evaluations should be mainly based on conformance to international UX design heuristic criteria like consistency, error prevention, user control, efficiency of use, visibility, language, and aesthetics.

To increase effectiveness and efficiency of usability tests, heuristic evaluations should be made prior to user observations and detected problems should be fixed.

Interviews Are More Effective than Focus Group Sessions

Since most of the software applications are used individually, one-to-one interviews are more effective than focus group sessions during usability assessments. People usually impact each other's opinion during focus group evaluations, and this deteriorates the test results.

Focus groups can still be organized to brainstorm the solution alternatives for usability problems identified during interviews.

25. What Is Requirements-Driven Test Management?

Surveys show that more than 50 percent of project failures can be attributed to problems in requirements gathering and the management process and more than 20 percent of them to problems in the testing process.

SDLC River

This situation can be best explained with a simple analogy from nature. SDLC (systems development life cycle) is like a river with requirements at its source. If you can't clean the river at its source, you will have a dirty river flowing down the hill. A reactive rather than a proactive approach to clean the river will increase the costs and risks exponentially.

The proactive way to overcome this situation is to formulate a requirements-driven test management process. To build this integrated process, the following best practices should be in place:

Independent Test Teams

The mistake of positioning testing as a last-minute, reactive quality control activity results in incomplete and ineffective testing of software. In order to avoid this problem, dedicated test teams should be established within IT organizations.

Business analysts and developers should leave the main responsibility of software testing activities to testing teams with professional knowledge on testing types, techniques, and automation tools.

To ensure their independence and objectivity, test teams should directly report to the CIO instead of business analysts or development managers.

Early Testing

Static testing activities should start in parallel to the requirements gathering process without waiting for completion of coding. Finding and fixing requirements defects on analysis documents after reviews leads to early prevention of failures in design and coding prior to the UAT (user acceptance testing) stage.

Applying early testing principles will also have a positive quality assurance impact on business analysis activities.

Risk-Based Testing

In most projects requirements documents are also used as test cases. However, test cases should not only contain positive scenarios but also include negative test conditions. Even in the use case test technique, the main, alternative, and exception scenarios in use cases should be combined with negative test conditions. These negative test conditions can be identified by applying risk-based testing techniques such as FMEA (Failure Mode and Effect Analysis).

To increase test coverage, these conditions should be tested with enough representative test data. Applying black-box test techniques like equivalence partitioning, boundary value analysis, and combinatorial analysis increases the efficiency and effectiveness of test cases.

Requirements Coverage

Requirements coverage is one of the most important test progress and exit criteria in addition to risk coverage, defect fixation ratio, and code coverage.

Hence in selecting test management tools, requirements coverage monitoring and requirements-driven test case generation capabilities should be considered as major criteria.

26. What Is the Role of Business Analysts in Software Testing?

Business analysts spend on average 40 percent of their time for testing-related activities.

They usually complain about this situation because they consider it as the main reason for not being able to allocate enough time for core business analyst responsibilities like requirements gathering, definition, and modeling.

No Escape from Testing

Business analysis and software testing are very interrelated processes. While business analysis is mainly related to defining functional and non-functional requirements, software testing involves validation of a system's conformance to these requirements.

Even in the existence of a separate testing team, business analysts' testing-related workload may drop at most to 20 percent. They still have a considerable level of responsibility, especially during functional, regression, and user acceptance tests.

Reviews

Reviews are a crucial static testing activity to assure quality by focusing on defect prevention rather than defect finding. Although design and documentation of functional test cases is under the responsibility of testers, business analysts should be accountable to review them in every project.

A test case design is derived from test basis and test conditions. While requirements form the test basis, associated risks and business rules form the test conditions. Business analysts should check that test cases cover both functional requirements and business rules.

A traceability matrix can be an effective tool used by business analysts to monitor and evaluate test coverage.

Impact Analysis

Regression testing aims to ensure that a change, such as an enhancement, maintenance, or defect fix, has not resulted in new software defects. The new defects may not only appear on the changed part but also on the integrated parts of the software. Testers should identify these interrelated parts and test them again.

The traceability matrix prepared by business analysts includes the dependency and blocker relationships between requirements and is also helpful in determining the potentially impacted parts of the software.

Coding Around Bugs

Running regression tests manually becomes time-consuming and boring as the number of test cycles increases. To overcome this challenge regression tests can be automated.

In an automated regression testing process, test procedures are captured as test scripts at the first test cycle and then run automatically in following test cycles.

However, test automation is not a magic way of finding defects by pressing a single button. Most of the time technical problems arise on test automation tools during test script generation. Fixing these problems requires advanced programming skills. For this reason test automation should always be the responsibility of technical test analysts rather than business analysts.

In some circumstances manual testing becomes more efficient than automated testing. It takes much more time to generate automated test scripts compared to running test cases manually. Especially in time-sensitive fast track projects, this results in a weird situation of coding around bugs instead of finding and fixing them.

Project managers and test managers should consider this issue as a project risk. They should mitigate this risk by determining the right level of test automation.

Challenge of Test Data Generation

Test data generation is another challenge for business analysts and software testers.

Most of the time, ethical and regulatory constraints prevent the use of production data. Test data have to be generated separately.

Automation tools that have data generation capabilities can be beneficial at this point. Using tools that generate test data by masking subsets of production data is currently the most effective way of facilitating this process.

UAT Is the Last Filtering Point of Defects

Even with the existence of a separate testing team, business analysts should be in charge of coordinating and guiding business units during UAT (user acceptance tests). UAT is the final stage for validating requirements and ensuring the fulfillment of business needs by the new software.

In case UAT is not conducted effectively, defects will be found by the users after the release, and this will result in money and reputation loss.

To increase the effectiveness of UAT, the first experienced-based tests should be conducted by business units without running any test cases. Afterward another UAT cycle should be organized to ensure enough test coverage by running UAT cases.

These UAT cases can be prepared by business analysts by simplifying SIT (system and integration test) cases generated by software testers.

Normally user trainings should be provided after UAT if the new software is replacing a legacy one. Users will be able to test the system in a more independent and unbiased way.

But, if the solution is a new one, then user trainings should be conducted before UAT. Otherwise, users will have difficulties in using software that is completely new to them, and this will result in lower test coverage ratios and longer UAT durations.

Long Support Periods

Following the release of software after UAT, business analysts usually have to support business units in using it. However, under normal conditions this support period should not be longer than three to four weeks even for large-scale projects.

A longer support period is an indicator of insufficient user trainings and a low usability level of the software.

27. What Is the Best Way to Reengineer the Software Development Process?

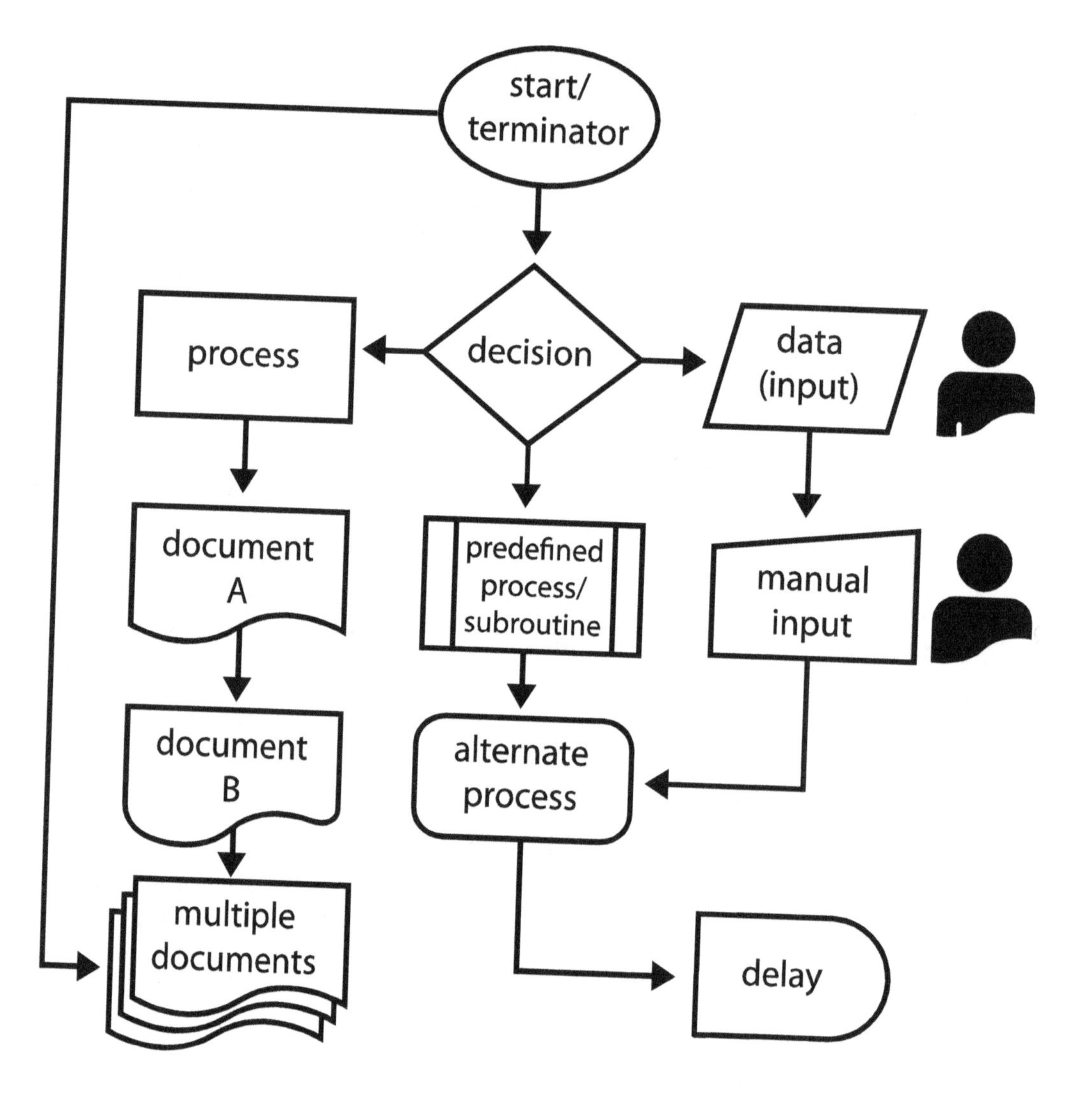

DNA of IT Organizations

For IT organizations their software development process has a similar role to DNA of living beings. DNA is the enabler of self-organization in cellular structure. If the body has a good DNA, it is healthy; otherwise, it suffers from diseases.

Similarly, the existence of structural problems in the software development process only guarantees failures rather than successes in the projects.

"Insanity Is Doing the Same Things Over And Over Again and Expecting Different Results" - Albert Einstein

After repeatedly failing in critical projects, most IT organizations reengineer their software development process. They search for the best methodologies, techniques, and tools to achieve sustainable success.

None of the standard methodologies like agile, spiral, or waterfall are suitable for all kinds of projects. Hence the new software development process could involve these standard methodologies but not have to comply exactly with a specific one.

The main objective of the new software development process should be delivering outcomes rather than outputs. It should produce workable results instead of useless documents.

The software development process should embrace change to adapt to future business models and new technologies.

It should also embrace competition within the IT team, because the high competition in the company makes the competition with the rivals much easier. Promoting performance by using measurable KPIs (key performance indicators) is the most effective and objective way of doing this.

Revolutionary or Evolutionary

There are two alternative ways of implementing a new software development process. The implementation can be either revolutionary or evolutionary.

In the revolutionary approach, the new organization structure and new tasks, methodologies, and tools start to be used as a whole just after the kick-off, whereas in the evolutionary approach they are applied as milestones in an iterative way. The Forming, Storming, Norming, Performing model of group development proposed by Bruce Tuckman is also applicable in the implementation of a new software development process. All of these four consequent phases are necessary for an IT organization to face up to challenges, resolve them, and start to deliver best results. Hence it is wiser to move evolutionary rather than revolutionary, especially in the transformation of SDLC at large-scale companies.

Rome Was Not Built in A Day

IT managers should be patient during implementation of the new software development process.

They should remember that "it is not the strength of waves that shapes the rocks but it is their persistence." Thus, they should continuously implement change management principles to manage internal resistance without giving up. They should act as role models and involve all relevant stakeholders in the reengineering process to increase their ownership.

Change Agents

IT managers should ensure that all employees in the IT organization have the awareness and understanding of the new way of software development.

Among all these people, business analysts and project managers have the most important role in the transformation of the software development process. They should act as change agents who motivate the use of new methodologies, tools, and techniques in their bridge role between business units and developers.

Index

CPSIA information can be obtained
at www.ICGtesting.com
Printed in the USA
FSHW020202030120
65675FS